Elise Houcek's *TRACTATUS* is a complete retaliation against material abstraction. It's unapologetic and loud, casting literary metal into stones and lexical stones into copper or ice. These deviating vignettes of Houcek: they melt. In August. They flash at us. In September. Today, they disobediently languish on the page of our eyes like a "slit of white duvet embroidered" on our "navy blue" reading glasses. With Houcek's work, everything could become impossible again.

    VI KHI NAO

Elise Houcek created a brilliant poetry page-turner in *TRACTATUS*. Allow your eyes to adjust to the breath placed between each letter and each unique insight between language and the lives that cannot help but speak it. *TRACTATUS* is a book we will be talking about with our friends for a very long time! Let's get swept into its vortex, from escaping interrogators to patriarchy's pronounlessness and a new meaning to chicken nuggets.

    CAConrad

TRACTATUS
Elise Houcek

Spuyten Duyvil

New York City

© 2022 Elise Houcek
ISBN 978-1-956005-13-4

Library of Congress Cataloging-in-Publication Data

Names: Houcek, Elise R., author.
Title: Tractatus / Elise Houcek.
Description: New York City : Spuyten Duyvil, 2022. |
Identifiers: LCCN 2021056556 | ISBN 9781956005134 (paperback)
Subjects: LCSH: Prose poems, American. | LCGFT: Prose poems.
Classification: LCC PS3608.O8495 T73 2022 | DDC 811/.6--dc23/eng/20211213
LC record available at https://lccn.loc.gov/2021056556

For Dana Bierma and Pamela Houcek

"A serious and good philosophical work
could be written consisting entirely of jokes."

Ludwig Wittgenstein

TRACTATUS

8 / 1 2

TALK TO YOU NEVER I said, and hung up the phone. This was not the first time my romance with Michael had devolved into a pattern of waking and sleeping, of closing one's eyes and then opening them again, trying and giving up. This pattern was in fact so reliable and dependable I began to wear it under all my clothes as a diaper of sorts. Most "respectable adults" (cue disc jockeys, cue hyenas) would cringe at the thought of DEPENDS IN PUBLIC but also be thrilled by the fact that a person has USHERED DEPENDS out of their private life and into the PUB(L)IC LIGHT, wretched but dreamy. DEPENDS IN PUBLIC comes in a variety of colors and sizes for all your perversed/reversed/ regressed/infinitessed needs. For issues getting your partner horny after he's lost his drive due to yours paying all the rent, we recommend the blue DEPENDS IN PUBLIC, said to have a diluting and calming effect. After your first wear, you may notice mild chafing around the midsection, but this will resolve quickly once you have settled into the new SEA FOAM OF YOUR LIFE. This will still be the SEA FOAM OF *YOUR* LIFE, however, so though it will be wet and frothy you will still recognize every bit of it. Look at it there, you can see the tiny face of your mother waving back at you as she bounces along with the waves, and there, your essay on Oppenheim's dorsiflexion of the great toe elicited by irritation downward of the medial side of the tibia, he's going to join your mother now, and way over there, way off in the distance, the miniature lamb you kept as a child and carry with you through every trial and celebration. All of these things are in their own way rejuvenated when you wear DEPENDS and are rejuvenated every time you hang up on your partner.

8 / 13

Slinking into that institution, the broken strap of my messenger bag dragging between my legs, I wondered whether the lights had suddenly gone out or whether I had been dreaming the whole thing. I had come to interview for a new position as a gatekeeper at the UNIVERSITY OF SEX AND ORANGES and was just as excited to finally get dental coverage as I was by the prospect of being harassed by these kids. Do not let anyone tell you otherwise, it is the primary duty of trolls, gatekeepers and crossing guards to present those who are crossing with a series of mundane tasks or to otherwise engage them. Here in the present paradigm RIDDLES no longer qualify as a MUNDANE TASK so it's basically my job to come up with an alternative, which usually involves being harassed by them. It's funny because I know I said it usually involves being harassed by them even though I am the one coming up with the riddles. But who, really, when we consider the topic of riddles, is the one being harassed, the one being tested? I would never say it was GOD or his magic capacity for PLAY but am interested to see how the speaker of the riddle is themselves A TARGET, how the subject gets switched with the object. Well, for one, they are assumed to exist in the SHAPE OF IT, a series of rings concentrically outlined so there is an obvious place to aim but many more to get lost in. I start to think everything in life is shaped like this. Then just as I'm drifting off onto that fine thought one of my riddlers throws an orange at me and hits me in the face. I don't take it personally but instead take it as an opportunity for explication (seeing the student's Intro to Essay Writing book in the back seat of their vehicle). "See," I say, "life is shaped like that, a fluffy miasma in which one can traipse around the millipedes and vines of one's own consciousness, followed by a bright kick back to aiming at the center, and these taking the reins, in turns."

8 / 1 4

Yesterday on the way home from my partner's parents' house I began to feel so tired I fell into a trance-like state in which I mentally reverted to the age of a four year old. I should tell the reader RIGHT HERE this story has nothing to do with any fetish or anything sexual and they should give up the thought of that RIGHT HERE or be prepared for serious or actually deadly disappointment. On the contrary, this story (I almost said satyr) has nothing to do with lust, the voluptuous, with passion, or with desire, and everything to do with its opposite, everything to do with boredom. Or with possession. As a four year old, it's hard to tell the difference between my feelings it's more like just EH>> Anyway, in this sleepy four-year-old state I became POSSESSED by the feeling that I wanted to play my partner's game (he was playing SPILL-THE-CUP-PEEKABOO-WHILE-DRIVING), but once I started I quickly realized I was not so much *playing the game* as *being played by it*, without any feeling or investment whatsoever. The game moved my hand in front of me, the game lifted the cup to my lips, the game dumped it out. Did I like this feeling? Yes, I liked it, even though it felt really weird to be so bored yet to be four years old and (what it seemed like) to be awake for it. Would I belong to this machine of

SPILL-THE CUP-PEEKABOO-WHILE-DRIVING eternally, without end? Now that would be a real fantasy.

8/15

Today I met someone who is trying to write a Young Adult novel, and I tried my best not to make any immediate judgments about what he is like as a person. There is very little I can tell you about him other than that his hair is red and he employs a particular method when he writes. LA METHODE is not particularly interesting or inspired but, I have found, works a genuine trick on the mind which, though initially appearing a detriment, ultimately serves as a great benefit to the writer. Here is just one of the benefits of modern dating. This man, we'll call him YA, only writes in his journal at the EXACT MOMENT that he feels he is THE AGE TO APPEAL TO YOUNG ADULT READERS (that he is in the exact mental state equivalent to a young adult's) and thus all of his ideas are entirely inspired and entirely true. There is only one problem, and that is he loses all inspiration by the sheer habit of the act, which moves in a diagonal line, crossing out the true youthfulness of his pen. AH, THE TRUE YOUTHFULNESS OF HIS PEN, I used to stay up into the early hours while he was writing so I could smell it, adorned with the lingering scent of fernstem and musk. I would go down on THE TRUE YOUTHFULNESS OF HIS PEN with such tenderness and vigor that I could picture a movie being made about it, and people actually did come out and start filming—the story of YA and his wife. Isn't that what I was? Though at

times it seemed like he was cutting
me, too, crossing out the true
youthfulness of MY life every time
we made love in the exact moment.
So I started watching us from above,
which turned out to be good for the
art, too.

8 / 16

Today I uncovered the primary source of envy. It has nothing to do with long, lascivious locks or wide, dun eyes and everything to do with one's apprehension of the relentless strike of time. A close second (I am prone to confuse them) is life's essentially comic nature, but again this begins to border on the Fallacy of Interestedness. I was watching this video of this girl, and she so deeply apprehended TIME'S RELENTLESSNESS (like perceiving this second doesn't actually move into the next and *I* am not really *I* because of it) that I began to think the most horrible thoughts about her. THIS, THAT, she said. THIS, THAT, THIS, THAT. It was like she was mocking me from the most infinite part of my inner being. Some people just aren't born with any injury, or they just don't see the benefit in writing from it...You know what, no. I AM NOT AN INJURED SOUL. I AM NOT A BROKEN OR HALF-PERSON, and I don't need any injury to write. I am god's infinite blip notmoving toward any ultimate destination, part and parcel with every living being, and I am not curious about god, like she said.

8/17

Mean as an automated baton I'm listening to I wouldn't dream of it by Joyce wearing a bucket hat that catches drops of rain while I gaze at the woman singing (she's hardly a day over thirty) and the way the sun catches on her hips I start to think I love her though I must remind myself this is no sybaritic fest. She flips her scrawny palm over, her bangles sparkle and jingle with the lightness of a celebration so close to the earth you can hear it stomp back as you dance. Beyond the white partitions severing the crowd from the dancers tiny black machines click against the light blue of the sky's seventy-two degrees and truss the stage together as beauty's performed on it. There has never not been a time like this. Vendors sweat in Pan's Jovial light, a flute's heard blazing out staccato notes over the land, promptly slipping into powdered goodie bags: little notes themselves. I feel at once utterly myself and infected by a land or people I don't know, ancient or modern, a tangent to my ken. I'm with a friend. Moving at an equal pace so our points are bound to cross we meet a man who invites us to his camp. The weather is about to break and we've got this fever to expand so we go with him. HAVE YOU READ, he says, THE TIBETAN BOOK OF THE DEAD. THE GREAT BOOKS. No he doesn't ask he says. To which I respond what of it.

8 / 1 8

Let's look at it like this: a KEN is not only a physical body, a type of preliminary gating used for rounding up DOGS or DOLLS, it's also a distinctly emotional body which can be thrust against other emotional bodies in an attempt to get something from them as in KEN I GET A _____ _____?

8/19

Today my boyfriend says one of the most interesting things, or rather this particular interesting fact of the day, which he is always eager to present before me like a spread of colored eggs, happens to be something I can make use of. Men are especially delect at bringing forward these kinds of eggs (indeed it could be said these are the only kinds of eggs they can bring forward). Inside each of them, there's a fact. Most of them bear no relevance, but this one did, which I attribute partiallyprimarily to our driving past the sculpture yard of the neighborhood folk artist when he said it. I think a little piece of metal must have broken off one of the sculptures and stuck itself into my sphere of relevance. I had never known the presentation of these facts could be a folk art of their own. It was a GEN Z fact, it was, come spilled from the rush of ages. "DID YOU KNOW," he said, "people in our generation read language that is properly punctuated as somehow inherently malignant/insidious/aggression-dealing? Like, if you use grammar, you're mean. I just think it's interesting something so decorous now means the opposite." HAH! I think. MY FINAL PROOF OF THE REVERSE OF MORALITY AND THE ETERNAL SUBJECTIVITY OF LANGUAGE! My black cloak rips across the windshield and I suddenly feel a purple kind of aquatic, animalistic. I have some kind of bill or I am carrying some kind of scissors, cutting up the scene like a sleuth. A little piece of my eye clips off as I'm traversing through the front seat swamp. WHERE IS MY BLACK LEATHER BAGGIE, my pencil bag, my clues, the only thing that can save me? I need it to get out of this swamp of quicksand and muck, this dream this joke this terror this charade of a front seat. At least now I know what I am. A platypus swimming-nay, lurching, scooping, threading through the muck. A cut-up scope. My beak's a cutting nose making meaning by accretion, attrition. Lay down the weapons of war (they all lay down). All the guns folded over on the hill. Into the grass with them now. Shut like a book. Down! I'm carrying my final proof. Another piece of metal from the sculpture yard breaks into my field of vision. I pick it up. It's a fact.

8/20

This is my job. I'm a clerk at a grocery store, and there are two things I love equally as much. So equally, in fact, I call them my regulars. The first one is the most obvious, and that is the colors and the shapes, the bimbo-ish, Platonic pure forms that remind me of the toys I use in sex, and the toys I used as a kid. That is, just being with them. The second thing I love most about my job as a clerk is something I got to do a lot today, which is write quotes down on small notecards and post them around the store (and sometimes even outside). You might ask if they are inspirational and I suppose they are but only in the sense that they are categorical and therefore usually precautionary. For example, today, I saw a pack of vaginal suppositories near the tampons and things, made for when one's internal grocery store leans too heavily toward yeast, and I wrote "DO NOT SWALLOW" on the lid. The box, of course, already said POISON. I saw a white, wide-mouthed mug with three categorical emoji-like monkeys and the line "HEAR NO EVIL SEE NO EVIL SPEAK NO EVIL" printed on it, and beneath that I wrote "IS IT IRONIC." I saw a birthday card with a watercolor painting of a boy in blue robes dancing through a field of grossly thin grasses blown by the disgustingly wispy wind and beneath that said "CHILDREN DO NOT EXIST OUTSIDE HIS ART." "IT IS, TOO, *WHAT* YOU CONCEPTUALIZE, NOT ONLY *HOW*" was the thing I wrote on the biggest card in thick, all-black block lettering and posted outside beneath the grocery store's name, which was something kitschy... Hmm...There is a reason why I have so many jobs...

8/21

You couldn't have rightfully imagined you would become anything like her or become her instead of working for her, could you have? We too had dreams like this but we find it so pleasurable just to be around her that we decided this was just one of those things in life where your agency is superseded by the pleasure of authority, of your smallness, your unexceptionalism, the orgasm at the hand of god's power. No one actually said these things to me but I could hear the whispers of them in the air as the famous artist gave me a tour of the production facility where I would work. I remember feeling excited, I remember feeling grand, when I learned I had landed the position. Now I hated the space between what I was and what she was—like she was the better version of myself others had always seen in me and hated now reflected in the refractory assembly line of her art. Her name was LEE. She knew something about California and people that I didn't. This knowledge allowed her to produce paintings that were exceptionally strange and relevant: the alluring trash/meanness of the feminine. OK Freud, you win, this dream is also about lesbianism. But had I not predicted this fall from my birth? I wonder...flipping through my earliest texts there is one painting completed sometime between the ages

of five and seven whose setting's
reminiscent of the one here, a
kind of factory of cells or parts
red stitch blue stitch blue stitch
triangles and squares rushing down
tubes and being carried across the
floor by green elves. Though there
is no err of doom. This is where the
refractory period of god is meant to
fill in the coordinates between two
dream images, but LEE has come in
to replace him. I hate her. All of
us girls working in the back have
to wear matching sweatshirts with
embroidered monograms on the chest
which you would think antithetical
to LEE'S revolutionary paintings
but the paradox of her image and her
ideal is, she'll admit, what made her
famous.

8/22

Dressed entirely in orange (orange suit orange cap orange wig) I squeeze myself into the brassy elevator owned at least in part by LEE's opulent caretaker, patron, husband, martyr, pimp. Numerous doors require numerous codes for entry which in my stoned state not unlike the dream of a Fanta girl petting an orange parrot I have not only forgotten but have been forgotten by, meaning I'm a radiant picture of a rat caught in the grossest and most opulent maze you could think of, and I'm ready to be anything but this photoshoot director. Alas, let's take a careful look back at the description of our character and what we find is I am not only a radiant picture of the color orange, I am a radiant picture of the color orange PLUS LEE. Who, what do you know, is the color purple. Which is just to say I'm a sliver in making a whole rainbow, which I have to direct! Then why do I feel so bad about it? LEE appears to have given me some special privilege, letting me direct this thing, letting me hang out with her patron-husband and her friends, though I think they might secretly be factory girls, too...but what I really can't get over, of what I really can't seem to get free is the whole ORANGE THING. We all went around and chose our colors months before the photoshoot was scheduled to happen. WHO WILL YOU BE and

WHO WILL YOU BE LEE asked us
each in our velvet, high back seats.
I DON'T KNOW, LEE said, IF THIS IS
REALLY A GOOD IDEA, I MEAN, WHO
THE FUCK IS GOING TO BE ORANGE?
Never again have I felt so hurt.
Orange, in fact, is the main reason
I admired LEE in the first place,
the main reason I admire myself. I
never knew it was so controversial,
though I'm learning this more and
more every day. It makes sense, I
think, why I work at the grocery
store even though I also work at
THE UNIVERSITY. It makes sense, I
think, why I so love kitsch. It makes
sense that I am like a white-footed
rabbit, aware of the futureluck of its
own death, of how beauty and disgust
are so invariably linked.

8/23

NOW I CAN MAKE CHICKEN NUGGETS!, I said, carrying/ caddying the red peppers I had just picked from the garden in my hand but really thinking *that is how it works, the one who becomes your nemesis begins as your friend.* It was in this manner I was able to go on churning out these deceptively branded thoughts, these "thoughts of revolution," by cupping a hot thing in the palm of my henna-styled hand while declaring the opposite nomenclature (i.e., chicken nuggets), all the while turning those peppers over like rocks in my mouth or glass orbs. Tick, turning, tick. Things growing slowly in the garden then I picked. And from that moment on the little red pepper robbed everything of its better name, having begun in the garden—the prime place to destroy a language and lose friends. I walked up the steps looking at them, they glistened with the impending doom and death of to whom they would be subject, the memory of the garden still glittering on the edge around them and with the tear of a fairy, and who exactly that doomed person was (or who that *particular* fairy might have been) mattered less than the sheer blinding color of them. So how did I imbue this food with a magical power, slip them into my partner's meal and kill him? Well, I already told you—I called them something different.

THIS is the core-end-culture of every CIA story, every murder, every story of redemption. Want to sell me a subscription to an investing app via refer a friend? Call it a chicken nugget. Want to send your ex a bouquet of flowers but not sure what to tell your friends? Call it a chicken nugget.

YA: This bouquet arrived / I felt like you were hiding something / inside / but I think I realized what I was missing was the palm of your hand, their insides pressed up against the crushed flowers' stems.

Me: Snip the stems over then flip them over the sink, run the water, dip, drink, what you see is pink.

YA: Mmm...baby (feeling a crunch somewhere in the middle, left part of his brain). I didn't know you had such shareable feet—I mean I know it's part of your bottom, but tell me about it.

Me (Signaling this moment / I might as well take it / the ribbon extends, revealing a bunch of them, red, in my hand): Had I felt this way before, I would have, but as it is this way, I don't, and I have a deep teleological response which bids me to usurp this—a queen's.

8/24

The precise moment the book shut, abolished the CO_2 in the space between the scritta pages, was the same moment she decided she hated books, not because of any real personal animosity toward the printed page, but because the girls she was most fond of in the story she had read had nailed the letter to the third-most peg in the loft of their parents' mansion, deciding it utterly secondary to THE BETTER ART OF ART AND MUSIC. THE BETTER ART OF ART was its own champion on the walls of the loft of the prettiest girl, we'll call her LEE, and all over LEE's body in the form of tattoos and piercings. There are other things I could say about the house of the book I am describing, or the people in it, and even more about the "she" who was witness to that page, but to tell you the truth I have developed an allergy to people and papers when they are stacked too close together. It's a pain, like the dermal needle writing LEE's tattoos. Too graphic or something. Too cured of oxygen. I go out to a lake where I can walk and try to put some distance back between the papers, back between myself, she, and LEE. There are only a few people walking along the lake and a dog that looks like a Doberman. I can feel the air start coming back to me, flapping the scritta paper in my lungs and in the trees. I come up around a bend where

I see the crescent of a back pressing out of a bush's foliage. My eye says LEE. How is she.

8/25

Ever seen a duck sprint? When I did, I caught just the tail end of it and it was like something I shouldn't be witnessing, something he was hiding, or like THE THE (sound of a steady) simulation of just-cracked videos blasted all over the TikTok app like technicolor sperm. Except this duck *wasn't technicolor*, wasn't showing off the feathers-fur-sppeeed of his rudder. So Nature's Bend and Snap? I don't know. He was the only duck around. Unless it was *me* he was trying to impress...though if he was, he failed, which makes it even more funny? While he sped off I got on thinking about myself even more than I was before his sneaky gesture, like about how I was in a manner thatduckinotherpeoples'lives, a kind of wake-against-the-grain or in their periphery, which they'd only caught the end of, attempting to break the blue and white starred paneling between us but really only making them think about themselves. Thinking, *well...If that person was sprinting, how fast am I going? How am I living?* The try, the glint, the falling asleep back into it, ourselves. And why else? For that is where the blue and white technicolor stars of our own heaven slide together in the mode of comparison or relation.

8/26

For it was not only you touching me that made my skin raise and my hair stand on end but the whole space around us *and* you. You and the crisp cool air collapsing out the air conditioner. So the thing we had intended as a "lunch" became like a book keyed to your pleasure and to the pleasure I felt through your pleasure. So while the entire universe in this micro-pan of universes seemed to move in our favor, as soon as someone entered our micro-pan (where we were, to some extent, being baked ourselves, albeit in a reverse direction, as the air was making us expand from its cool. But, more than that, we were eating food), things felt slightly contaminated by them, like they threw our universe off-balance, and suddenly what was a kind of pure pleasure to which our whole world answered grew dark. It had something to do with them looking like the worst future versions of ourselves. I knew it, you knew it, so did the man, but the woman, she might have known it but held on to something dismissing any relation. You were like her and I was like him. I noticed things and so did you but you didn't let them get to you. They felt like a drop of food coloring in the pan which in a way disturbed the water but also made it more interesting. I solved the problem of judgement.

8/27

What do you mean by front? I didn't know what you meant by front. My body was so tired, I went to the door instead of the window. I don't know why you're laughing, not funny, I say, or do not say but think, my body so tired I cannot spare to speak, but I can imagine, along with the upward strand of my thought, a little medieval devil like in gibberish's paintings ramming his horns into you. Ever think I went to the window instead because the window represents a plane separating me from you, and this devilish thinking? While the door represents just enough space to insert a text box between us, oddly shaped just like the little devil with his head and points? And the fern beside my window by my bed. And the darkness outside. And the sound of your laughter the only thing one can hear for miles, echoing off the license plates of the cars parked on the streets, the people sleeping in their homes. In what other stories has one appeared to another to bring some trouble though appearing well-intentioned? I know there are many. I've seen this trick before. But for some reason yours feels perfectly designed for me, all your maneuvers and gears and even your way of laughing now is how to get me right between my will and my want.

In another scene, he's mapping the cartography of my head with his chin. I'm meowing. It hurts a little, but it also feels right, like in this style he cares about my tired body, wants to caress it, albeit to make a map of it.

"I'm OK with maps," I say. His eyes gleam.

"I could ornament the entire crown and still you wouldn't recognize a queen."

"You attempt to bring some good intentions even though you are troubled. I like guys like you."

He slips my hair behind my ear.

"Well, yeah, my mom loves me. And then I went off to school and learned everything I know."

"And you started selling pendants door to door?"

"Yeah."

"What did you wear?"

"You mean while I was selling them?"

"No. Now."

"I have them under them."

"Let me see. What color are they."

He pulls down his white elastic sweatband to reveal his emerald green tights.

I turn my head away from him and say *you know what they say...*

8/28

Before the plot thickened, before
we imagined THE MYSTERY OF
CRINKLECUT as our *own* creation, he
came to us in the shower as a spur,
a spontaneous eruption in the water
that showered us in its je ne sais quoi
like a citrus scented bathroom mist
or like a grass catcher dumped off
the lawnmower and emptied. I can't
remember if it was fruit or emptiness
that was the dominant feeling of
the meaning, but I do remember how
hard we were trying to remember
that word's meaning. *Crinklecut,
crinklecut.* As soon as you said it,
I'll admit, I was afraid. It felt like
a part of my brain I had lost the key
for. Is this what it is like to have
Alzheimer's? I feel like I may never
recover! Although I don't fully mind
(I don't live in THE FULL OF MINE
MIND) this new spaciousness because
I can stretch out really far, my
long legs like Popeye's girlfriend's
extending in a lawn chair in the
shower (which is where we were).
We were talking about crinklebear I
mean crinklesmut who keeps tipping
her hat up to the right while moving
to the left and kicking her leg. She
keeps leaving. NO!!! we say. NO,
CRINKLECUT, DO NOT LEAVE US! WE
AREN'T READY! It's not that she *is*
ready it's that she just doesn't care—
she's like a machine going going
though we want her to stay. Then I
say, WELL YOU KNOW WE COULD
JUST *GOOGLE* "CRINKLECUT"? And
that's when I truly understood the
crucifixion.

8 / 29

"Oh!," I said, like a little mouse friend, dropping my bobby pin on the shag where it stuck perpendicular in the mat. This unexpected moment of synchronized favor / utility pointing up from the dirty / white shag in the dark black of the bathroom, the black of night

I can't do anything for it : the light fails it zips

itself up but isn't beyond : the bathroom's proclamation

I had to sneeze : I walked to the light outside my window

A streetlight as if a moth : to a lamp my nose up like a mouse

I called it "embarkation" : and the waves felt made out of

"Edison's station" : a technicolor sperm current

I didn't understand : why I would be leaving tomorrow! I would

throw it to the wind wear : my hair without a pin!

Edison wanted to come in : like the old man in my dream

I wanted to fuck him : my boyfriend set me up with him

The reception was fairly interesting

8/30

I didn't feel warm yesterday. I didn't feel like buying an "option soup." Since high levels of T in women contribute to an overall sense of being able to curve the world toward you, I was surprised (also probably an effect of my high levels of T) I could have such little interest in what was usually my favorite part of the day. I walked out into the yard and saw the grass was kind of yellow. Of course there was no soup to buy there and that is why I decided I must go out in it— the immediate motionless optionless plain of my backyard...that would do it for me, yes, rearrange my hormones so I would again be interested in things? Like a tarp which when laid out begets the many iceboxes of a campsite? OOOOH I would reach my hand in and *choose*. I could do it right now, actually, this grass does not desire a pitch, and I would be close to my house and all the creature comforts it contains... soap, soup, mom and dad. I thought I was depressed, I just needed to camp!

I thought I was depressed, I just needed to camp. I brought out all the kitschiest gear and props I could fit in my red wagon. Some arrangement of them made me feel good for the moment, which was a long one, at least in comparison to the day before

when not even soup felt like an
option. The mean sun looked down on
me like a piece of construction paper
in an empty sky; an eagle flew across
it and ripped it to shreds. I looked
down at my arrangement of hats and
plungers. I realized the things I had
been trying (or maybe the sun was
only fake until I realized it, and it
ripped when I got the point?) were
in fact NOT creature comforts—there
was nothing I could do with them!
But starve in the vanquished field
of mild yellow grasses stuck all like
little lowercase l's pointing at the
ripped paper sun, mumbling l l l
love, l l l loser.

8/31

Do you ever look at something completely random and feel quenched of some unquenchable thirst? Like do you ever just lay your eyes on something and that something lays on your eyes back, so it feels like that something and your eyes are cuddling, wholly and interminably? Well, I have, and the same reason I felt it is the same reason I will never leave my home in the Midwest: lawn ornaments. Little glass orbs and statues of Bambi, a wagon or a broken Christmas tree set up in December, things that aren't meant to be lawn ornaments but become them, a pink sand bucket, some chalk. I like them especially when the weather's cooling, when there's less and less greenness on the trees, plants. The other day, the second I glanced at a particular one of these houses, one that loves to do the lawn ornaments thing (this one, I think, had a fence), I felt somehow I had forgotten all fear of death, and I could exist forever curled-up in that sleep-warm space. No, literally, I had forgotten all fear of death–I was really, truly, fundamentally safe. Random, I know, but the more I think about it the more I think maybe that safeness is in fact part of an equation. I still know my elementary maths. I take out a pink pad:

9/1

1 + the loop, the "bamboo cinquain" of my cul-de-sac – the normal force (carry the one) EQUALS some lawn ornament-type spirit that equates the support of a good family with a clustering of material things. But didn't I have that? (I look back at the question... It says something about there being less and less green). OK, I'll add that...

1 + the loop, the "bamboo cinquain" of my cul-de-sac – the normal force (carry the one) EQUALS some lawn ornament-type spirit that equates the support of a good family with a clustering of material things MINUS the greenness on the trees, plants, EQUALS an indulgence in the fetish object, which, through its simulation via pigment, resists the season's natural decay–a "win for capitalism." So all of this together gives us the tragic answer that my eyes and that something were never actually cuddling.

9 / 2

For it was a way of winning out, a
way of "beating" that was not so
mired in the world of the physical,
such that when a member of one of
the teams went ahead and "exhibited
their reach"–i.e., clobbered
the other, with the girth of an
outstretched ruler–the sleeve of
tatted ink revealed once their cotton
sleeve delicately flipped back,
recoiling to the force of the wind
from the punch, was actually how the
winner was determined, not by the
force of the impact, or rather, not
by the force of the *body's* impact,
but by the force of the impact the
sleeve had on the eye. People began
to engage in these displays instead
of handshakes, the winner determined
by how far back the sleeve blew the
competitor's eyelashes. The last time
I was involved in one I got so tired
I let the force of the wind on my
eyelashes completely knock me back,
such that I was sitting on the little
green hill, leaning back. I breathed
in the milky air from off the sea. I
could see the shadow of YA's figure
in front of me. And from then on I
decided I would keep a list of other
such hypodermic distractions.

LIST OF HYPODERMIC
DISTRACTIONS:

Similarly, something else came to be used instead of force: a competition known no other than as WHO CAN HIDE ONE'S HAIR. And do I think my predilection for wearing hats as a sign of status is related to my high testosterone levels? Yes, but this is hardly new information, I've been wearing them since I was a baby. WHO CAN HIDE ONE'S HAIR is played only by the most beautiful and independent women–the ones who, like LEE, have never dated because they are just so "picky" which means they haven't had their "break" and so are kind of robotic anyway (hence the style of my language)...It is like this triangulated game of sexuality: to say "I conceal my feminine powers via a bowler" and "I conceal all feminine bowlers so you, men, think you have a chance at striking out" at the same time, confusing the meta-sports. I remember the night my hat actually won the competition, beat the other girl who was DJ'ing. The same night you asked me to dance in something like six or seven years. You really whipped me around. It felt like I was flying through the air.

9/3

If I could just get one more sip
if I could just imbibe in droopy-
fashion a corner of that "world" with
my retina, then it all would fall
into place, then I could continue,
reinvigorated—I could live! But what
world? It looks a bit like this one
but is less well-tied. It says things
like "spilled my 30th cup of tea so
I hope I meet that new love!" and
"the regression therapy is surreal,
but I'm less crabby" and "website
coming 8/13/23!" If I could have just
a small bite of that language, I knew
the sugars would get me, or blast me,
through the night.

People eat people eat things. This
is why it is so cool to have SOUP as
one of the motifs in your artwork.
This is why LEE does it. It suggests
not only that you are comfortable
with slushy items but that you
recognize you yourself are among
them, positioning yourself as the
most inappropriate of approachable
artists.

There is nothing soupy about the
world or art I want to take a bite
out of. Well, there may be *the
presumption of soup*, a kind of
liquid arrogance, but nothing *really*
suggesting a post or even mid-
digestion state. There is just a
raw, vegan parading-its-hardness,
which must be where I get all my
ingredients to make the soup.

I go back to the profile and start
scrolling through the page, thinking
about how nice of a meal has
been laid out for me, all in their
perfectly square containers, a small
ingredients list conveniently beneath
them, some even color-coordinated.
I break off a piece, just a corner,
like I'm marking a page or a tab, and
consume it. It is cold and starchy.
Probably not good for my low levels
of T, but it gets the job done.

9 / 4

Listening to Mos Def in the most jealous arrangement, I puffed home fuming re: LEE had more clowns in her home. His lyrics were my attempt to distract myself from the red nose and carnivalesque costumery reappearing in her house in such subtle yet equally varied and pronounced locations (on the shower door, in the potter next to the television) that it was as if form and content had made the perfect arrangement (or had eloped and nobody cared about it), since that is *exactly* what I thought clowns were good for—I puffed— their subtlevarriedpronouncements. I just kept "swimming along" as I walked home, a little tune I oft' repeated when there was something I had to get through. I did it a lot in high school, though lesser now, and even as I realized this, my steam continued to rise until I was a kettle about to sound. Fitting *imago theatrical*, I know.

What a purge I was of the pain and egoism of capitalism, I mean what an overflowing example of it, which I could somehow rationalize as being related to martyrdom, since I was displaying it in order to purge myself of it. Clowns were like that, too. That's why I had to have them.

The lyrics kept pounding down my ear into the slimy wet puddle that looked

like face paint. I was listening to
"Speed Law."

When I got home, I made tea. I
thought it might reverse what was
happening to me through a form of
sympathetic magic. It did, for the
most part, but there was still the
tiniest whistle squeaking out my
holes, almost worse than when I
was screaming red. No, I was like
a gnat whose violent power was all
contained in its projective ability to
maim, its foreshadowing. Well that
was what was really happening here.
This whole feeling and everything
you could say about it, everything
leading up to this point actually
had nothing to do with the clowns
at LEE's house or my jealousy of
them but was merely coincidentally
aligned because there was some
other, more meaningful event to
follow this?

I was grateful!

God had given me the gift of endless
change!

9/5

She really did look like an artist. Comfy cloth the way she dressed the way she walked somewhat ghastly. Her Tinder date standing at her door's step, well *he* looked like a model. Me closing the door behind. I was the real artist, tea in my hand. Tea in my hand, tea in my hand. No soliloquy was ever so wrought without that good, plain accompaniment. Mint, consistent like the fuzzy stream of pink pleasuring my headphones and the light green color opposite...What's it called... complimentary? About this word I couldn't tell when it was applied to someone other than myself but by someone like me...To tell you the truth, I could hardly see the difference between myself and my closest friends, unless, of course, I got real close and spied the lines between the pixels. I'd look like a mouse or a creep, nose parallel to their nose and a quarter of an inch away from their tucked-in plaid shirt, driving. Our lives were like driving on a giant, plaid sheet, always and throughout all eternity. We were giving ourselves to a higher order that throbbed with the ambivalence of a drugged-up teen, noble on the one hand and totally self-interested and detached on the other. It pulsed with the heart of a drug. It stuck its flannelled hand from inside the cafeteria stall and slowly turned over to unspeak the

potion. Whether what it promised was
taxes or substance we couldn't be
sure.

9 / 6

All day I've been fucking writhing having a good time watching someone not being themselves on an app called Fish on a show by the same name. That was, until our fight. I told you my headache was seething back there, keeping time like a four-by-four barista in an underwater schema like a reef with an orange time-keeping thing—a stick…What's that called? A baton? Not this trope again. But keeping time, either way. In his pocket like contraband. I'd totally scene'd this—you calling yourself "poor" instead of just admitting you were lazy, my headache frothing since, being so on the edge, I can't admit that what it *really* should have been called was close-involuntary-womanslaughter. That's what made me sick. An eel frothing on my chest. And to think all women go through this? And some don't even escape scathed. Once I'd let go of where I thought the story was heading, I was able to escape with only a few breaks (once for humorous and once for certainous). By that point, the only images I could invent were totally dissociated from their context, like the one of me, my body fumbling down concrete steps and my arm breaking in a disembodied, prickly space. I wonder if that's what Rothko meant when he said, "the rectangle is the symbol of our age." But here we are in the TikTok Era…

9/7

WHERE IS LAKE EERIE? is a question I often ask trying to sound cute while simultaneously uninvested in any form of originality since it's a question not only I ask but every clerk in this grocery store is forced to ask, when they get their turn. We keep under the cash register in a cookie jar fifty folded up scraps of paper with questions written on them, which the management periodically turns over so customers don't get sick of them. They all sound like this, which gets my hypothetical dead ancestor turning over in their grave, a weird mixture of earnest and dumb, so even if I wanted to graduate from the high school that keeps me at a job like this, I couldn't. I haven't learned to conversate in any way other than what even the most outsider artist would flinch at calling a "bimbo retrospective." That's what THEY tell me. That's not what I believe. I believe it is a way of keeping an eye on me, of controlling me, and what a regular proposition to have all the other workers get it on it. But at the same time I kind of like it, and it fuels me even more, just vocalizing these dumb questions, just uttering them with my mouth, forming my lips around those round syllables? Ugh, it's almost like when I ask these kinds of things, all I hear is the echo of my voice fluttering like a fish or a kite back into my own face.

We have the perfect environment
for it. You can come down too, and
we can listen to it. A white-walled
gallery performance.

9 / 8

The two of them (me and my friend) end up on the other side of the fence the night that's mostly spent shepherding, bringing each other bread. It was the only place the sun wasn't beating down right on us since the pre-production bureau had come out and cut the tree line back. TOO TEMPTING, we thought, and I convinced my friend that that thought was deserving, moreover, that *WE* were deserving, not only as people but as creatures who pulled out our names all night. ANGEL was one of them. YOU'RE MY GUARDIAN ANGEL, she said, smearing her hand across the imaginary screen existing in front of us simultaneously. We could see it though nobody else could. We sat on the ground in the dead grass eating mangoes outside our van while a couple of men from the 6 AM WAKE UP GAME periodically passed by. We looked at them not with our eyes but with our heads, not saying but silently confirming that we were indeed still passing through 5:55 AM. So, as angels are wont to do, we went to sleep under the branch. I woke up to my little friend hissing in my ear (THE SOUND OF IT), then two red-clad women on Clydesdale horses (THE IMAGE OF THEM). One blocked the sun that warmed us. "I thought I could just pretend to be asleep!" I told my friend later that night, after the Clydesdales had taken us

back around the fence, an obscure
iteration of the walk of shame, back
to our camp, which was just two
feet from where we previously lay
resting. Two patted down patches
remained, like where there were some
sleeping horses. Of course I *tried* to
hop back over, my black silk chemise
and silver sequined shawl catching
on the fence's one part, but I heard
my friend call me back, beckon me to
head back in. I followed the rules.
We were back in the game.

9/9

STOP WORKING AT THE SOUNDBOARD!, I shout. I'M DYING! But my voice from the stage you're at is too far away, and the sound of people partying is probably all you hear. I, on the other hand, am up in this tree, in the woods on the periphery of the festival's farthest stage, which, when a group of people aren't taking it over for some event, transforming the grass into a green slab from which metal objects shoot up at various angles and a giant black tablecloth's made to make the stage, is just a farmer's property. Clearly, everyone has forgotten that this is an actual WOODS, equipped with WOLVES, so believe me when I say I was just as surprised as you were to have found myself pursued by them. I'm also surprised by how far I can get up this tree, and then by how much *farther* I can fly up the trunk of this tree, which has become slippery, paradoxically aiding me. Which is more than I can say for my phone, which I am somehow still managing to text you on? The product of which I can't say you don't receive because the connection out here is weak or because *our* connection out here is weak. There was that one girl you bought a drink who you said was your co-worker during set-up...So I keep shouting. YA!, I shout. YA! Now somehow the dogs are becoming increasingly manly. Veritable MAN-DOGS. LONG

AS LOGS. Maybe I'm just in Paul Bunyan's time, and you're in yours. I think that's what they say. Love's just a mirror of yourself, and any disconnect has to do with time-space?

9/10

Now that I have this tracking app on my boyfriend's phone, I am starting to worry about what it is doing to me psychologically. Not that I'm worried it's making me a creep or an obsessive-e-girlfriend or whatever—I'm concerned because I'm starting to think of the tracker as a fundamental law, applicable to whoever I'm next to, talking to, playing cards with from behind the glass. The other day, I was with my friend (WHO I WOULD NEVER WANT TO TRACK FOR ANY REASON! I LOVE HER!), and when she stopped paying attention to me for a minute, I took out my phone and I tried to look for her! It was weird. It was unconscious. It was bad, I know. Or was it subconscious? I had always struggled to tell the difference between the two because they both start with the same letter "u" and so I decided must be equally subjective. Finally, I deduced, this has nothing to do with *her* or with *u* and everything to do with the patriarchy's pronounlessness. How all men slide in to hijack your temporal lobe's repetitions, so you go on stuttering the same word, their name, leaving you destitute of all other syllables and unable to speak to your friends. A wedge between women and women. Two interpretations of Eve. Between women, however, there are differences, too, tending toward the

drastic, like, I'm remembering now...
some friends willingly track each
other. I need some of those. We could
wear pink gloves. We could modulate
modernist panels on feminist love.

9/11

In LEE's factory, all of us girls utilize different HEADER TECHNOLOGIES, which is how we preserve our difference which is how we will remember our names. Some girls use footers instead of heads, some girls put their footers on the right, some on the left, some girls put their last names and some girls abbreviate. Like K.M. Martra. It seems utterly dis-romantic, I know, because it is so graphic, but, for one, LEE is obsessed with paper and pins, and when you really start to think, it's actually the most romantic thing to protect yourself against cosmic forgetting. *We know that's why LEE makes us wear the monograms* (a phrase one can often hear scaling the white brick walls behind small groups of girls on their lunch breaks, especially behind me and my friends, K.M. and one other new one). And every time we fight against it, it's like an Egyptian blue lotus flowering, which compliments, ironically, LEE's new yellow Lotus Elise. We have started this new thing where we are secretly collecting copies of all the girls' header technologies and doing group exchanges so we can compare them in private, see how deserving we are of LEE, ourselves, and each other. The first time I saw K.M. Martra's, it looked like this:

          k.m.
        Martra

(At the bottom of the page). Almost immediately I began thinking so radically differently, I felt like I knew K.M.'s entire history and had forgotten my own, but somehow it was all okay because it brought us closer together? And a flower bloomed in the space between? We went on comparing in this way as an act of solidarity, the antithesis of LEE's obsession with paper and pins.

9/12

"There is nothing greater than the recognition of oneself," he said. "And THAT'S what sweeps the boundary between learning and envy. So it should be said in spite of them being born with the cards stacked in their favor, they operate from a true space." I could hear his video game clicks as we talked over the phone re: how I would get my life back together after the new job working for LEE. I wanted to love her, I did, but I questioned whether a man who could afford to drink Original Almondmilk with his non-mint T was capable of giving me any real advice. In a word, he only read the most general books: LBLC, the I Ching. Up until this point, I had done no learning or I was on leave from learning, so I never cared about its connection to my little green man, the fourth sin. I should have believed those books the first time I read them: learning's bad. From here on out I will give up all of learning's extras and the movie will continue as a low-budget biopic, the way my parents intended. That would be the move, so I could operate the camera from a true space (right now, it roves, is handheld). Plus, I'm sick of them in their split hem, glittering, flared-leg jeans. They insist on perpetuating the fashion of the time of my birth, the nineties. A visual reminder of the stylistic errors of my childhood self which persist in my life because of their presence.

9/13

Of course I have to whittle it down,
the thought which is why is my
generation so playful, the moment
I drive under a yellow stoplight
(cameras beholding my ass) and start
justifying things. Actually, I think,
I don't know which is more true!
Of the Generation In-Vests (some
from Goodwill, some from Jean Paul
Gaultier): whether we are driven
by the hypertrophy of the intellect
or by an underground playfulness/
playlist that exists unknown but
rife somewhere. I didn't come up
with these terms, and I wouldn't
put them together either. I mean,
I wouldn't be the *first* one to put
them together. That's the other thing
about Gen Vests and our relentless
collage aesthetic—we get all our
ambivalences from reading books.
And we put them back there, too.
Yeah, we like it when things return.
Look at my white pleather I mean
pleasure lime green Gaultier spiral,
spiraling across my legs to where.
To where we all, no doubt, first
acquired our detachment as *playfully*
self-conscious: our CHILDHOODS and
our MAGNET SCHOOLS, where, like
the little bugs we kept in red, arched
bug houses with cut, bent screens
(*CUTE BENT SCREENS*), we looked
out at the world totally-blithely
unaware of our own cush green moss
and how it would one day poison us.
Only *our* cush green moss was our
color-coordinated magnets—the return

of lime green in the present–meant to
teach REPELLING and ATTRACTING,
and our BUG HOUSES, and our
ABACUSES, and Jean Paul G. We came
to school wearing vests. We read
books. You try to repeat that.

9/14

I FUCKING KNOW THIS PLACE.
It's the UNIVERSITY OF SEX AND
ORANGES. I know it in a way
that slaps me over the head with
the hardness of an object that's
consistently metal. Before, I hadn't
been here, and this place was
strange but stranger now's the all-
of-a-sudden irreversible intimacy
that stitches the buttons of the
UNIVERSITY into my skin almost
as if it were a person I don't want
to break up with. I come around
the bend (I FUCKING KNOW THIS
PLACE), feeling closer and closer to
the recognition of my kin with the
rising motion of every parking gate.
My words belong in parenthesis.
The parking gates rise and fall
frequently but out of sync, beating
the air into a frothy substance like
I'm whisking eggs or snubbing at
the sea. Searching for underwater
trove of treasure? Smell smell
smell. No one else around. At the
same time the air is choppy, it's
also calm and cool, quiet enough to
hear a peg drop, but totally empty
of anyone else, which means I keep
losing my scent, consistently. This
has happened before. I have known
a place, previously. I come across a
random assortment of leaves that is
a leaf pile obviously blown there off
the road in the corner in the dead
grass and an old woman who's just
hanging out, just wallowing in them.
She looks depressed. She's breaking

the leaves into tiny segments and
arranging them into a message,
massaging them. At first, I think,
I don't want to fuck with that, but
being so lost already, I roll down
my window and ask for her help.
I ask whether this is, in fact, the
UNIVERSITY OF SEX. The letters
she's arranged look like they spell
MEAT PLUG. Her hair is dark as
licorice and her heart is somehow
exterior to her, drawn in a muddy
red. It is my own grandmother. She
is a stranger to this place.

9/15

"I need you to take me back to my camp," he says. "I'm scared," he says, "that this will turn out to be an homage to youth culture." "Don't worry," I say, "it won't," and I start gathering my stuff, most of which isn't useful: a glowstick, a bag, the scarf my preschool teacher bought me in India. I'm not sure my phone's in it, or I am not sure if it is that my friend will have a phone for me to reach him, just like I'm not sure how the sun will ever reach this vapid field of grasses covered by droves of humans without an ancestor in sight, in the middle of the night, in the pitch of midnight, tents pitched out by the parking lot with their various flags and tropes, inflatable dummies brandishing memes to scare the self out of the body and into the ecstasy van where you can get fucked by one of them, then laugh yourself out of that van, too. The same glottal stoppage between the in-breath and the out-of-breath running vampant running fear in the eyes of this boy who's stuttering and eyespeaking for us to take him home. As we walk, the festival blares and though I'm glad I'm not experiencing it now, last night I was, or I was experiencing it through the friend I came here with (this guy freaking out is just a guy from the neighboring camp) when she got scared listening to sexual house music. I understood she felt the universe's feeding after her. By the end, she and I felt like we had invented the word SHEPHERDING, not that I was shepherding her but that for maybe two hundred years no one on planet earth had been stripped of and given the exact right conditions. Things were reversed now, but with him. We went back to our Lot.

9/16

I think we are all just scared
so somewhere else in the world
someone can be less scared. It is an
arrangement based on illusion but
also on compromise, cooperation and
love. By this I do not mean we step
into the machine simultaneously,
that it's signed, sealed, and
delivered before it's ours, before the
other, more scared person becomes
"ours," I mean there is a kind of
PLUNGERING UP or PLUNGING UP
that happens automatically when
you do eventually integrate with
them. Either way, the position you
come to assume is a little rickety,
never mind the surrounding tulips.
So it is like through our entire
lives we are swimming, for always
and eternity, and the plunger is
another of the sickening ways we
are woven together. So we depend
on each other in the most profound,
essential manner, yet also in the
most illusory. But perhaps I am
applying the regular feeling of
freedom from the fair rides I took
in my childhood? They have not
only *impressed* themselves on my
subconsciousness but can be said
to have *written the very script for
it*, every dream and death-fletched
vision having something to do with
plungers now or conforming to
the shape of them. I know this is
common. I went to the doctor, and he
said other people experience this,
too. I thought his answer would

make me feel better, less scared and alone, but ended up, as usual, just making me feel totally unspecial. Dark as night against the fair's neon.

9/17

I walk out onto the earth. There is a patch of grass showing through the snow where the radiator's wires heated it and melted it from. I say to my friend, after she tells me her car is headed for the junkyard, I *AM* A NINETIES MUSTANG. And that's all ye need to know. I've plodded out onto the earth. It was a permutation of itself, sporadically transforming into a derivative made from the leftovers of the first earth's kitchen. I wonder if the kitchen is connected to the radiator, and whether that radiator, in turn, is connected to me—so it makes sense my friends think what I mean is the antithesis of Nature, but au contraire, I mean wild n free.

9/18

LEE has me do things for her even when she's not around. COVER YOUR MIDI PAD, she says, YOUR MINI PADS, SO NO ONE ELSE CAN SEE THEM–I OWN THE GROSSNESS OF YOUR FEMININE. By "gross," LEE doesn't mean sexually inaprop., she means anything that shines a light in front of strangers. I look at the lights on my pad, shining off the water. I live in a second story apartment on the river with a balcony let out by two sliding glass doors so when a boat or ship passes by during the night the lights play off the glass like they are happening inside. There is one night I keep trying to will the lights back to, in June, when a small party bus with a neon green strip made its way down the river and I got to watch it crawling across the black screen of the glass doors in the mid-air heat as I lay on the couch falling asleep. It was like everything I had never dreamed of all happening while I was alone. That's the problem, LEE gives us rules to follow while we are alone, which, sure, you could say other companies do the same thing, that it's part of the regular nine to five, but it's different with LEE, with LEE it's tactical, hypocritical, almost. She tries to disrobe us of any iota of self-worth to be gained through the very things she relies on in her art. I lie on the couch, missing the way my midi pad's lights used to play against the glass as if they were the neon green strip I loved that singular June night. Only the pad's were rainbow and mobile. RAINBOW AND MOBILE, I think, wondering if this is a way to get around LEE's work-home ideals. It's girly, sure, but not gross in the same way. A Death of a Salesman feeling's headed my way.

9/19

I'm radically reapportioning familiar
bodies/deciding whether I should
use them as a shield or protect, only
asking this question because my
fear makes me flinch, opposite the
reason I got into this mess in the
first place: my outstanding defiance
when that gross group of men hit on
me. We were at a bar or some bar-
like restaurant in a town I didn't
know the name of, me and three of
the four people I love most (it all
loops back around to the portmanteau
of the father, his letting go), when
these old men said something crass,
in unison, their white hairs and
leathery skin making them look
like old, dead books. I think, THIS
ESTABLISHMENT WOULD BE BETTER
OFF STASHING THEM ON A SHELF
(or using them to cloak the outside
of a portmanteau), so I summon all
my feminine rage to respond, AS IF!,
or something along those lines. I'm
hunched over my plate, though my
noticing's speckled out, fitting its
little tentacles into the air's bloated
suspense, which circles around
one of them in particular, the man
closest to 35, probably. Idk. Men
around age 35 who hate women tend
to file that hate into the sharpest
screwdriver because they have their
eyes affixed to never being able
to fix one good thing again? No
bookshelf. They want a little friend.
Well I won't be that. And I feel the
rage of the last 400 years of my life

spuming out when I respond to them. Some will say I should've saved that rage for a hate that affected me personally and not have spent it on those strange men. Some do not understand the light I feel when I hear a woman I do not know utter the words "feminine rage" in a sentence. Alas, that man shot me, or tried to, and the whole time I spent sliding the people I love most in and out of the way like a duck-shoot carnival game. It felt like the whole dream was about me or something. Like the dream WAS me—a kind of map. And these random numbers (400, 35) were actually measurements that represented my psyche and my body. As if from them one could build a house.

9/20

There was a fish I saw it laying there. It was on the table. It looked like it had been prepared lovingly and with care, though it was, visually–and we must admit this– something sore, a silver lump on a silver rectangle. It divided the house according to gender, though no one could quite articulate how. I think it had something to do with the women's failure to transform the fish's duende into care, so instead of coming to dinner on our knees, we came to dinner laughing. We came to dinner laughing and the men couldn't understand why, figured we must have been poisoned or swept up by our new community, overjoyed. Come to find out we were laughing because of the fish *AND* because of the new community, which did feel kind of slutty, but the air we breathed was well and good. For years following this event I would remember the fish and what it did for our factory, *what it did for me* (I keep a picture of it on my phone that pops up periodically every June), and hold out on the theory that the fish was a gift from God. At least how it appeared.

9/21

Sitting at the coffee table today
(the table inside the coffee shop,
drinking T), when I use a word the
wrong way: *IT FEELS*, I say, instead
of *IT SEEMS*. Though its usage
isn't temporary (i.e., it wasn't a
mistake), I catch it, write it down,
and hurry up thinking how much
more this is than a trait. THIS IS A
LIFESTYLE, I think, I want to say
to my friend sitting across from
me to whom I recently gave advice
re: her boyfriend, tagged with the
suffix *IT FEELS*. When I look down,
and fondle my tea bag as anyone
with empathy will do, the message
swirls but *IT FEELS IT READS IT
FEELS*. Such an easy loop it should
be tagged with an emaciated star
referring to my college scholarships
page. It moves slippery-ly, is a
good page. I want to rise out of my
chair, shout it to the world, but
resist because of Dead Poets Society.
Because if I share something that
is true privately, it had better be
done without any cinematic tugs or
toboggans. I want to be free, to be
a lung slashed out and pinned gently
to the tree, to be, as it were, *LIVING
SILLY PUTTY*, a vowel ripped out of
its aeiou counsinry. Which is why
I say it feels. Which is why I am
excluded or removed by two degrees,
though still technically related
to the vehicle, the tenor, and the
family. Mama, however, was a bass.
While she played, I watched her as

a young child. It seemed our little
family was performing a limited-
budget script, which immediately
felt like we were living it, in it,
and the budget was only moderately
limited, it seemed. It was all green,
the foliage around her. The air that
bodied the rucksack stage we built,
and no one ever spoke in metaphor,
hence I learned to say IT FEELS.

9/22

We are in the car. Driving toward
some open field where we will cram
and park our car. Rub sunscreen
on our necks, heavy with rocks
and silver metals. Michael/YA's in
the front seat, switching the first
letters of words in phrases not so
that they mean something else but
so we stop thinking about the words
and only think about sex. That's
our motto: no words, just sex.
BATER WOTTLE, MRAIL TIX...or, no
words without their objects! YA's
secretly a devotee of William Carlos
Williams, just like people who break
sidewalks are devoted to them. It's a
practice done only in the car on our
way to events (I wear the same scarf
to every one, and only that) since,
once we get there, we are entirely
objectless. We swing in the hammock
and watch the spider spin its web. As
we jump down by the marsh and the
crabs, only once do we think of death
by MAIL TICKS.

9/23

Today while I was on Tinder, someone asked me ARE YOU A TRAVELLER? I wanted to say of course, we all are, but there are some important ways dating a man changes the way you do THE TRAVELLING THING, for that is what most dating app bios are really doing, they are meant to be taken as WARNINGS, they are meant to WARM this recipe to a specific degree: "THE --ING THING." Dating people (and especially blind dates) is like placing each aspect of your life into the microwave, one-by-one, individually wrapped. Like anyone, this guy who asked didn't want a general answer like YES or YES. So I said, "I am someone who has done the travelling thing in these two following ways," drawing two light blue crinkly oval-shaped containers of food out of the microwave (one, of course, contained something smashed, at which I winked). I lay it down and showed it to him. "The first way is independently, without you or anyone else. It's scary, sure, a little spicy going down, but I eat it feeling like a total connoisseur, I eat it enjoying my food. The second way includes you, is still friendly, but, after a while, might start to gross both of us out. I just lean a little back like this, and you lower the food down my throat using a gravy boat." The food is brown, like the boat. That is what it will be like...you and me doing the travelling thing...cutting through the calm, brown waters in a boat in some Italian city.

9/24

GET THE FUCK OUT OF MY KITCHEN
+ HUNGRY JACK tell the story of
my life or at least impress the
stereotype of the last six months:
a cliche + a cliche = a cliche. On
the one hand, I am consumed by a
Khalo-esque rage accompanied by all
the fertile power/fertile flour of
the "pits of the fruits" cliche, and
on the other, there is my slipping
desire (like the towel that says
GTFO on the stove) to welcome my
boyfriend, to cook for him. I hate
that I am subject to such universal
irredeemable pitiable patterns,
but I am slightly disoriented, or
slightly re-freed, by the simple
fact that there is room for variance
within that equation, for a kind of
pollution. So even though Francis
Bacon's bloody paintings reddening
the room's air have been thought
of before, probably a million times
over the course of the earth, they're
still special, revolutionary actually.
Both the same as and radically
different from the bright red pancake
box I'm examining now whose
godforsaken milkwhite lettering
suggests yet another red, spangled
over a second packaged product of
violent capitalist exchange, only for
hamburgers this time. Both the same
as and radically different from the
actual color red. So time doesn't
really move, since I keep shooting
back and forth between dumb
repetitions. It has a floury texture.

9/25

Here we are again: crunching through a LEFTOVER-PIZZA-WRAPPED-IN-A-PRODUCE-BAG-WRAPPER-IN-ANOTHER-GROCERY-BAG FEEDING SITUATION. I say FEEDING not because I want to say RABID DOG but because I think it is one step removed from SURVIVAL. And I don't want to say *that*, not because it isn't true, but because it's TOO WORN-OUT. Here in the TikTok era, we're all about NEWNESS, which requires this kind of FLUX, returning to PIZZA BAG WRAPPERY like WTF, I'll be glad when this is over...

9/26

What various things, such as OVER-BRUSHING, such as WRITING, such as pinching your finger into each individual tooth crease so as to feel a good kind of pain ultimately make you feel really tired afterward? Drug dealers, for one, especially this one, who's the cousin of my best friend's boyfriend and whose affects cannot be differentiated. This is the only thing about him that reminds me of myself. When I'm along for the ride in the passenger's seat and we're driving past the sculpture yard, I don't do anything but stare, out the window, out the front windshield, which is where this drug dealer keeps looking, now, or so I think. He's actually looking at the screen, into me. IS THAT RADIO FENDER'S COLD BLIMP IN TRASH?, he asks, not looking at me since I'm driving. "Yeah, it is," I say, "but it's turned down, so I didn't mean for you to hear it. It was just 'up next'," since my therapist told me to write a letter this week to my younger self. And he's so much older, I think, 37...maybe 38..and he doesn't work, AND (I could have said I was doing research, telepathically, which is why he only saw the song's name, but I care even less than him). AND here's the point. He just breezes over my non-responsivity to say, YEAH, I FUCKED WITH IT BACK IN THE DAY, I GOT MY L-PIN, BUT IT'S ONLY GOOD WHEN YOU'RE

WATCHING THOSE PRETTY GIRLS SPIN SIMULTANEOUSLY. The more he attacks everything about my former self, the more at peace I feel. It's like he's jabbing his finger again and again into the gums between my teeth (with a bit of nail), and I'm gliding into a snow-colored, undifferentiated field as we approach this turn. I've fallen in love again.

9/27

Another evening walk with him in
this frenzy-ornamented town. Another
lapping lag while on the sidewalk
as my blood huffs to get the baton
around (too much coke, too much
sugar in the break). We pass, among
other things, a statue of a lion, who
guards the right edge corner of the
small white house's driveway. The
statue of the lion is weirdly shaped,
as in it's got its legs folded under
it, as in it's lying down. I wonder
if the lion's posture is contingent
on the kind of home it plays in front
of (mine certainly is)–when I'm at
LEE'S, all my back can do is lie
down and breathe, since it's not
random that she has those things.
This house is random, too, but
not the words I sent to you while
noticing that lion, or that that lion
sent to *us* in the space between our
recognizing. *Guarding*'s the word.
Guarding's got fur. As in it came
to us in the space between. As in it
deputizes the Land of Nod(t) (furry,
sleepy children nodding out with
the gesture of a paintbrush amidst
granite spires, sighing, the gesture
of a mouse. Baby blue Snuggie...
baby pink...). So you were saying
the lion was doing *not* that, v lax in
front of the port-style house with
its trinkets parked in the loading
belt. Also, the lion was granite, and
so didn't have any fur. I wondered,
or was wondering, after you pointed
to the lion weirdly not-guarding his

home, his friends (might as well have pointed into the air) looking for a word to describe his failure, NOT what word should be filling in the gap but whether it was worth mentioning at all. Whether you were worth it, this breath. Plus, I wanted to save it for myself. I discovered it, I unearthed it in its real beauty, which was not its clicking into this particular question but its clicking more generally.

9/28

After taking my vow of silence, there are things I want to say but can't, most of which take place in the shower, which previously had been our site of greatest intimacy, delicious mutual exchange. Now I just shower alone, and a quick reddit search on the monk community page, anyway, says this is best. It also says time will be affected, either expanded or shrinked, as a consequence of vocal powers shifting. Mine shift in the direction of the fast, which I am privileged enough to experience for the first time via a sculptor's perspective! Monks of reddit say you will experience identities outside yourself, too, which I initially brushed off as reduced but now I'll tell you I'm enjoying very much, I'm enjoying my time here very much now, yes. Anyway, I experienced them for the first time via a sculptor's perspective when the soap bar I got newly minted as a birthday present was placed not duly enough out of harm's way (I think, *what got me into this silence game in the first place...weird placing*), and so the water rapidly hacks into its body. So rapidly I enjoy watching it dying. I finger its dying body with my hands, it reminds me of the coconut creamer I put in my morning smoothies. Which reminds me of you, weird lover. How I want you to understand how much I love it (the coconut, not the soap, since the way I stick that is almost always an accident). But instead of understanding, instead of even attempting to understand, when I ask you to lick the coconut creamer off my finger, you say, "only if we fuck first." It is my greatest loss, my greatest disappointment. It makes my vow of silence realer since I'm now absolved of the shower's recourses.

TODAY

I gave up all my charms. Now, on Friday nights, I go to the grocery store and my charms are the soup boxes, the people I see when I look around. I go with my boyfriend and buy him a little treat, something bubbly but uncaffeinated, something with tropical packaging. DO I MEAN DEATH IS MAKING US GET INTO KIDS' STUFF? Kind of, but not really. Its aspect ratio is kiddie, but the pixels themselves have much more sheen. They let things slide off of them, like a plate, the plate on which I serve dinner to the children I'll never think of having. Sometimes I wonder if this is the real cause. That it's not just death's fault? That I might actually live in the world again, go out to parties, etc.? Our bubbly water could be caffeinated. Cruel trick that all cool women will have to face. All women whose faces lag and lapse over the pixelated cart BECAUSE THEY HAD SOME BRIGHT IDEA. MOMMY TOLD YOU NOT TO DO IT! Mommy showed you curdled drinks! But I was too young, a baby who was already a baby. That's enough, I thought, and went back to sleep. I went back to sleep since I was the child and the mind of the child at once, since I was just a touch away from snuggling bliss. Mentally. Physically (I looked down at my cart, then my boyfriend, whose shirt was surely fleece). I told him I wanted us to consider this a date idea. I wanted him to consider that I had come up with this idea and what that meant for us. I had a sneaking suspicion that he himself was into the tropical treats idea, but I learned as a child that men aren't into sticking with.

TODAY

You shouldn't flirt with strangers unless you want your dad to end up dead. It was a dream that taught me that. I've been having them repeatedly, featuring outlaws in reverse, where I am the outlaw and some older man drives by in his car and fuck! shit! I wink at him. I wink at him, and he gets out of his automobile. My fear is real, because he's about ten times the size of my dad who is small for a man but has the heart of a tiger. The heart of a tiger is the feeling I get the moment the man's affection switches to violence. The moment our eye contact precipitates his reaching for the handle of the driver's seat door. He looks like THOR. My dad and I were just lying in the grass by the sidewalk (I think we were ourselves outlaws), taking a break from running from the men who've been interrogating me, running from them even in my dreams. This must be their new intimidation tactic, their bluff of tall men. I feel the cavernous bluff behind me, caved in, the grassy part on which we are standing. The man I winked at is automatically shirtless, has long hair, and proceeds to pummel my dad into the fractions that we are. I keep having permutations of the same dream, so my questioners are obviously trying to stay sneaky, to slay my intuition, to invert it, so I can no longer trust my most private moments. It's perfect. I mean it's my geometric kin, this sewing pattern of men trying to murder me just after I make eye contact with them, just after I return the favor. So there is no darkening rope I can follow in. I can't investigate the investigation.

TODAY CONT.

Driving home from the grocery store when I think (this time as a customer and not a worker, though I've still got a piece of paper with one of my interrogator's ditzy questions written on it. It fizzes as fast as I can think, the actual speed, in the back pocket of my jeans, contributing to the scene's texture) no one in the world could possibly understand the rhythm, I mean, the texture. My life is just too private! Do *YOU* know what happened the last time I went to a flute lesson? Good, cuz you'd think less of me. The rhythm and the timbre. We do have Google now, which I have associated before with the light of God, how it can de-empty space for good, sic save ourselves from Alzheimer's and oblivion. But what if you don't know what to look up? A classic problem. In fact, I'd say a universal problem, essential and newly evolved like girls skateboarding. How about the rhythm of the train. It is such a unique sound I do not think any words could be used to describe it. All I know is that it's rhythmic. That's all I know about most things, since I am just a bug or a leaf vibrating some progress across the pavement. Unprecious but cute. Writing is this way, too, that's why I wear bows a lot, especially when I'm at work. Okay, but. The weirder thing has nothing to do with rhythm and everything to do with the order of things. For example: I roll down the window because I'm feeling hot and let the snow fall into my car and onto the black leather I let the snow hit my black leather after feeling vertigo from losing my vision amidst the train cars passing and the sound of shrieking and rhythmic breaking. OR I let the snow fall into my car and on the black leather I let th e snow hit my black le ather

TODAY

At the gas station, grabbing the squeeze, which worse than my ouched-thumb (cut on a book) reaffirms my body's/tail's/fuel hole's being simultaneously puckered and mechanical. Which is sex. Which is death. Which is the way the first does the advert work of the second. Mine, this week, is blue, with subtle flecks of a brushed-tin sparkle complimenting the gas. However, here, no luck can save me. No man can scratch-off this scratch... though I will still fuck him since aslongasIhavethisheadandaslong asIhavethisfleshandaslongasI paintthesenails, I will not be celibate. I will do the good work, play the game that's good. *AS GOODNESS?* No, but I did temporarily, for the one to fifteen years before I fueled myself for the first time and knew what driving felt like. That's when I played for that team. Now, I live in a pond of oil that glitters as you swim deep. Did you know, all over the world right now, approximately 8,000 pounds of nail polish are being swallowed by all kinds of people, rich and poor, as we speak? Little chips. The most anti of the anti-abstract being consumed readily and unreadily in moments of rote anxiety. I get in the car. Turn on some house music, which I listen to rotely but not unreadily, passing by the coffee shop where I used to work. So many palaces. Recently,

I've been thinking about writing an essay on house, its relationship to nail polish, orifices and death. The next song flicks on. It's called *Des-i-i-i-i-i-ire*.

DAY

THIS GIRL DOESN'T GIVE A SHIT, one of the guys says, who's camped next to us with his friend. THIS THIS. It turns me on, not to be made into an object but to think of us as iconic–he wants to murder me on a spiritual level, and that is precisely why we will go far together. THIS GIRL DOESN'T GIVE A SHIT which translates to THIS GIRL ISN'T AFRAID OF DEATH, OR ME KILLING HER? IMAGINE THAT. He is like my Christmas flyer, my onliest patron saint, who, upon beholding at the time of my death, will help me ascend steppingly into the next realm. Though right now he steps on me, I know the favor will be returned. YA only wishes he could be this person for me, but the only thing they have in common is hair and a guitar, with which this guy, I'll call him Michael, sits in the flatbed of his truck, as if on a little cliff, playing for passersby like an aloof bard in narcissistic green tights. Our narcissism, previously unmatched, is why we have this fling. I had a dream we were rotating together at the bottom of the stairs once, dressed as clowns. I decide to do something nice for him, to show him I really do care, that I'm not so out-of-town. I break off a chunk of something, kept in an old tea carton I bought in college where I have a series of droppers another man gifted me. Then, maybe an hour later, I ask for the gift back. I couldn't do it. I could give him myself, let him ruin me, but when I think that the whole thing could have been a fantasy? A dropper of what I had to give I just couldn't make good.

TODAY

A few days ago I was driving down the highway not feeling zen when I realized the plant of all the greatest problems in my life: I am too grateful. This plant, though small, was already large enough to be grafted and thus made its way between various obstacles of presence and absence. Made its way through the grate without realizing all the energy expended in going both ways, in riding it, my salt-encrusted blonde hair flowing freely, in chunks. And now I was just tired, so every time I made a turn (even the meek one, now, on this gentle highway called a road), the life went out of me a little more. In the spot I'd weakened, my stem was torn. I went to a doctor who specialized in plants. He also specialized in dogs but for some reason was taking a break to specialize in plants. He said I was special as soon as he saw me.

"Why?" I asked, "because of all the tears in my flesh? The purplish bruise that's shining, almost wet, against the life-affirming green?"

"No," he said, "because I've never seen someone, or should I say *something*, so life-affirming. You really let it have fun with you in bed, didn't you?"

"Doesn't affect my present."

"Sure you do." He took out a licorice-like potion and set it on the desk, the counter—whatever, the doctor-thing.

"Codeine?"

It was something different. With a variety of sounds I could have named it. LOVE-POTION, FORGIVENESS-POTION, MILD-POSITION...but as soon as I took it, I forgot these, along various other words. I straightened up promptly, and my stem felt good, but when I looked at the doctor we no longer tingled which was much worse.

DAY

I walk up the stairs, my high levels
of T affecting my right down to my
underwear, or my underwear affecting
my high levels of T. Problem is: I
can't let it burn. Millions of women
have walked this ride up before
(albeit with roughly four times
less T) which is CARRYING THE
LAUNDRY/ HAULING THE WHOLE
LOAD OF LAUNDRY up the back
steps leading from the river to the
apartment. Yet, it is not my back,
but my burn that's spurned. My fire.
Not in a theater, but my ability to
shout fire in the woods, to save
the animals and deer and to hear,
projected and echoing, my own voice.
HAHA, yeah right. This has nothing
to do with woodland creatures and
everything to do with MITES, MY
FAMILIARS, who gather wood for my
little fire. Which gets too big.

TODAY

My high levels of T and new job working for LEE have made me obsessed with a new thing: the simulation of reward-risk. And I do mean the simulation of it. In other words, I'm obsessed not with the actual *outlining*, of things-to-be-lost and things-to-be-gained (for example, buying an optionless soup from the grocery store, understanding this involves its own cost-benefit analysis—and what I mean is you can either die, Ponyboy, or you can live) but with the transfer of energy implied therein. So I bought the tomato soup with the red pepper integrated. Nevertheless, while I was going back and forth (while I had tomatoes and red peppers in my one hand and a PACKAGE OF HORMONE PACKETS, a PACKET OF HORNS, in the other), a strange feeling came over me. It sort of felt like reading a syllabus before your class has actually started. I mean it felt like a tingle having nothing to do with the immediate moment other than the conjuring up of everything that could or will have happened, past or future. So in a way I was committing *everything*, all my present will and energy, to some space and time whose value was a figment, just like every time I write in my diary I'm expecting some unimagined reader to read it. I love the feeling of an absolutely dumb exchange which gives you no proof for your money.

DAY

Another dream, or no, another conversation at LEE's factory. In this one, some of us factory girls are assessing the value of wharf imagery in paintings, or any imagery that suggests "urchins." At the end of the conversation, Factory Girl #2 doffs her hat and makes a toast, a weird but subtle reversal of social mores that somehow feels so nautical, as in it swerves, just like Ambling Peg Leg Joe. Factory Girl #3, however, has decided wharfs are soo not what LEE would want, much better to be worn by Jeff Koons, who by the way LEE's friends with. But why not? At least LEE trusts us with these kinds of branding decisions, I think. At least she knows *we* know exactly what kind of ship's wheel she'd be rendering if she was doing it all by herself, what kind of wood. I ask the question again, quickie-dreaming-up a magazine page from a child's nautical-themed bedroom in Pottery Barn and thinking hard about how I could fit all those things into LEE's newest painting of a sedan's black leather seating.

Factory Girl #3: LEE doesn't give a fuck about people, or their parodies. She has a version of herself that's often tennis-playing, but that's only because a small part of her *is* that woman (She draws a Venn Diagram, or a bubble map, one of those two).

Factory Girl #2: You mean wharfs are just for boys?

Factory Girl #3: Do *you* mean wharfs are just for boys? (She knows Factory Girl #2 is right, and she feels sad that some part of her agrees with her, that she is, for some traumatic reason she can't explain, lying to herself. *I can't help it*, she thinks. *I'm cheap. I was raised that way*).

Factory Girl #2: Okay, dude, fine. Let's pretend it has nothing to do with gender. It's a totally different element. This is WATER we are talking about, not air, not earth, not light, WATER. You thought LEE's secret flaw was that she sometimes compromises quality for quantity? She's a rich girl. She's Type A.

DAY

DO I CRACK IT. DO I CRACK THE DOOR: one of the most important and recurring questions in the history of this planet. And the follow-up: or do I just keep delaying the debut of my full form, as a kind of battle strategy? It's worked before. I think of quantum entanglement, for one, and how I would do anything to protect me/thee. I decide to go with halfway. Halfway because I'm into youth culture's dialectic of discipline and play. And I'm type A. THIS COULD BE DANGEROUS! PEOPLE HAVE GOTTEN SICK! I have to keep reminding myself of this throughout the course of my life because sometimes I forget dialectics themselves thrive on laws (cause and effect, transfer of energy) and aren't just games. But, alas, what choice do I have, I leave the door half-cracked. A whiff of sulfur curdles up from the pile of laundry on the floor, mixed with patchouli. When my friend gets here, the other friend who she said she was going to bring isn't even with her, which leaves me feeling pointless about the whole thing. My bedroom, or no–the slit of white duvet embroidered with navy blue flowers–languishes there in her absence.

NIGHT

Pressing the bulb in the corner of
my eye, a bird got caught in a snare,
a flare, skittered, then I lay back
down and thought I would never get
up again. Then I lay back down into
the white of my bed's turf, down
through the square of it, the plane,
then down again, through the sheets
of clouds, the elevation changing,
turbulence sans. I would never return
to work again. Would that be change?
Or would it be anti-change? Inertia?
I preferred to think the latter, to
feel dead momentarily, though still
fuzzy. Here from my Saturday-
morning casket I watched various
phenomenae of the eye play in front
of me like seeds in the air and a
giant red bar of light. Like SCENES
IN THE AIR. Like *DECONSTRUCTED
TABLEAUX*. How do I do that. I
recall the people who have used the
term, summon/re-imagine them in
my mind like ancestors travelling
in a great backwards-flowing line.
XUAELBAT DETCURTSNOCED. The act
is noble of itself and light enough
to sustain Semordnilaps. Is that my
name? I do a lap around my sea-bed
backwards and upwards-facing, arms
outstretched. The names of teachers,
mostly, come to me, the names of
all my dead teachers. They fall into
my open mouth like gently dropping
fruit and taste, mmm, like cherries.
Cherries mixed with cream, so less
red than pink. O yeah, *XUAELBAT
DETCURTSNOCED*. They're trying

to teach me something. To unteach?
Every time I swallow another one,
the scenes I watch in front of me
on the bed become more and more
meshy, less opaque. But no sooner
than I think the word MESH, someone
whispers YOU GOT IT, then I'm dead.

TODAY

There is a dog who gets picked up to move over THE SNOW-COVERED SIDEWALK. The SIDEWALK is a kind of thing that suggests the VIOLENCE OF THE UNIVERSE, the DOG'S PARTITIONING. And the fact that the owner's hair is the same brown as the dog's is the sly smile of that arrangement.

NIGHT

My ceiling fell into my blender. My incense fell into my Lay's Poppable chips. I took a picture: warm to the touch. LEE would love to make art out of this, I think. Would love to sink her fangs into the touch, but I won't let her, I won't archive this. And hence, in not-archiving, paradoxically this is where the *real* touching-of-corners begins: experience! Like a bird in the woods touches a stick. Usually, LEE would force us to record these things, every aspect of our private lives that she could somehow make use of in her art, especially the things that have the subtle meanness of her paintings of the insides of cars. But I won't do it, not this time. No. I've been a new bird since February, and, being transformed, I've finally decided to leave the space in front of my kitchen sink and go out into the woods, to really live. I will take no camera either. So the entire time it will be like I am leaning into the world and in no position to step back and criticize it. I travel into the woods, leaning forward at a thirty degree angle. I will touch every corner I can. Intricate. I won't document any of it for LEE's online blog or her sketches. So that's what I do, I go into the woods, gingerly padding up to anything that looks slightly wet and gray and poking it with my finger, the secret suspicion that I have been working in LEE's factory for far too long, that I perhaps have forgotten what nature even is, always already behind me. Always already leaving what I will become. Always already the breath that is my archive's antithesis.

TODAY

When LEE is young, she has photos of her friends she tapes to her wall. I do not understand it. I mean I cannot wrap my mind around it. I sit there, wondering if it's something *I* did, like maybe I have less friends. But no, they are THE OBJECT OF MY MOTHERLY DERISION, my OBJET PETIT BLAH, not because of what they represent (the faces of a few friends) but because of what they deem is absent. Or because what they deem is absent I somehow cannot understand as good. CREATING A LIFE? YEAH RIGHT! I have no future-orientedness until about this time, which I trace back to my father, who, unlike LEE, knew nothing of California, nothing of being free. Her wall is a pea lime green whose oppressiveness jilts its inhabitants into doing nothing other than playing dress up (is this why I can't wrap my mind around it?). Checking your phone...I watch LEE tape the polaroids to her wall; there are hardly any of me, not even the time we dressed up as spies on Halloween and put vodka in our squirt guns. I want to say this to her, but I don't. REMEMBER WHEN WE DRESSED UP AS SPIES, LEE? REMEMBER WHEN WE TRICKED THAT GIRL'S PARENTS? Instead, I ask if she needs any help. Do you need any help, LEE, taping your friends to your wall? I like to do this, or maybe it's a habit I was born with,

whenever I feel sad or excluded
asking to join in with it. I remember
LEE likes pins as I lift a pink one
and put it in my mouth. Suspicious.
I wish there was a color in this room
besides green. How old are we now,
twenty-three? Most of the pictures
are of her at festivals. I've been to
a few but not enough in large groups
and I'm still more of a child than
anything else.

TODAY

"You look the same," he said. That's on Michael, I mean YA, who can't often be found purchasing charms for his Do-It-Yourself earrings at Michaels or Hobby Lobby, but you sure can find him at the Guitar Center next door, which is arguably much worse. Now, it's his roommate's turn. I think he studies econ/is too smart to be going to the UNIVERSITY OF SEX AND ORANGES. "You look," he says, rubbing the crust out of his eyes while gaming. "You look like a sexy hentai character, like Sailor Moon. Like Sailor Mooooooooooooo-n. Do you know who Sailor Moon is? Do you know who Sailor Moon is? Hey, YA, your friend looks like a hentai character, like Sailor Moon." But YA's already playing his guitar, crying in the corner amidst empty bottles and remote controllers, amidst only that. The next one takes his turn. I don't really feel like I've consented to this, but it's like I think they're too dumb for me to waste my breasts, or I'm just too tired in general, already really abused. "No, no! She looks like a really flat surfboard with a sharp, singular fin." I Google PARTS OF A SURFBOARD on my phone. For some reason, the only one I can imagine my own face on is periwinkle. I get a strange kind of power thinking about that. Yeah, the Sailor Moon one sucked, but for some reason I can get behind this. I wonder if I've

reached my true form, and whether
I owe some debt to the particle
boy who came up with this one. He's
definitely as cute as YA, who's in
a puddle now in the corner, just
playing his guitar. If I fucked him,
I'm sure we'd recover.

10/14

There is no truer test of friendship. Can you say *THAT* WAS KIND OF... OVERWHELMING when recalling a traumatic event, then, following the briefest of silences, laugh with your little girl friend. I had a friend who was the opposite of LEE in every way and we performed this test together, daily. It was a GIVING-PERMISION on behalf of us both that made the traumatic event more scared of us than we were of it. My father used to say this, while we were at dinner eating steak, at the same restaurant I used to frequent high on acid reading *Flatland* by Edwin Abbott. And I actually thought for a second that that Edwin was somehow related to the one for whom my friend's mom worked, making drugs and sleeping in her cubicle overnight. Which is another way of saying I was reading *Flatland* for how it appeared in MY life and not for the dimensionless-planed-serfs or other romantic notions. My father used to say, while we were at the table and I was burping things unrelated to food, "If you're going to read that book, you better make sure it's more scared of you than you are of it." AND STICK WITH IT. NO BRITNEY SPEARS SHIT. I might have heard him wrong, but my father was always oscillating between two perspectives on control, one minute suggesting I was a bug, de facto, and another minute commanding I make that bug be me.

My girlfriends were the only ones who understood how that was funny. My girlfriends who were small. The ones who wore tight, lacey shirts and island-themed bronzer. And later actually moved to an island. The Big One.

10/15

In a way, I want to be able to say
I've gotten my L-PIN, too, not so
much to actually *wear* the charm
on my lapel, but just to say hey,
I got it, and then I threw it away.
It's a LONG-GONE L-PIN like my
fourth-grade rabbit's foot charm
is a LONG-GONE MEMBER OF THE
LEPUS GENUS. It's a long-gone
MEMBER OF MY JEANS/MEMBER OF
MY GENES–my father, for instance,
could continue wearing his L-PIN to
this day and no one would question
him or distribute any blame. So I
brag about the charmlessness of my
bag not as a way of putting other
people onto it, of assuming any fame
(unlike my friend's cousin's drug
dealer, who attacked me for playing
Radio Fender's Cold Blimp in Trash)
but to say *I have broken the horrible
cycle of the generations. I've lost
the charm, for good.* I mean, THE
good. I look back at my friend, who
I can tell wants me to summon the
phantasmagoric oobleck of my charms
via describing her boyfriend as a
really sugary drink. "I know you
know the life," she says. "And you
do not want to make it worse for any
of us, so you stay at your house, you
don't try to have your birthday party
at my boyfriend's house while his
kids are around." My rabbit's feet
have detached from my belt loops,
and lay around my feet below the
couch in a kind of fairy circle. It's
weird, I want to give them to her,

but it feels like trying to CRISPR yourself into somebody else's jeans. We're both wearing light-blue, pinstriped, flared jeans. My couch is also gray, which is enough for me to begin to count her as family.

10/16

All of us girls, while studying each other's handwriting, come up with a list of things LEE is bad at. When we're huddled together doing this, the monograms on the backs of our sweatshirts bounce off the metal vents at the factory's heights and make like Britney Spears' SOS. Or a signal to the wolves, the dogs, the moon, anything chrome. We come up with the first one. LEE is horrible at signing things with somebody else's name. She could never send a text or a meme followed by another text that reads "From, Somebody" whose name isn't LEE. This is pathetic at best, deadly at worst. We know LEE doesn't let it get to her, since she's making so much money off of paintings of the interiors of cars, but we do think it demonstrates some internal pain which we could potentially monopolize, usurp in the future. We hate that we're just pawns in this power game but it's better to be a pawn than a board, or an empty box, I say. The other thing LEE can't do, via a kind of myofascial release, involves the fundamental problem of consciousness. It's not that LEE can't imagine other consciousnesses existing in the world, otherwise her art wouldn't be so good, it's that she can't imagine another consciousness imagining hers as the All. We write it down: LEE can't imagine the All. The factory is growing more and more red, more and more brick-full.

DAY

Today I discovered a new technology from one of the bite-sized communicable squares referred to when talking about the girl who's launching her website on 8/13. It's called HAT ENERGY, or something along those lines, and as much as it came THROUGH ME, it also came OUT OF me, which, we can admit, is true of most technologies. It came through me and also out of me/from me, each time, in the form of a small square, a little tablet, a Listerine pocket strip, since I've had HAT ENERGY since my birth and have always been good at naming it. I brought my foot up to my mouth while wearing a pink one, for instance, which this guy on TikTok can't really fathom, now, can he? I would like to think he'd challenge me by adding to my sense of what HAT ENERGY can mean, that he might make use of his time by presenting GEN VESTS with a full symposium on the technology's new interfaces, but the problem is not him, it's me. The problem is I don't care to change, which is the veery HAT ENERGY kicking in. Though at the same time, HAT ENERGY is totally malleable, constantly in flux? It feels slightly harmful and performative at best, like a much bigger problem than can fit it this tablet...

But if it's constantly in flux, can it cause any real harm? I think about this often, especially in relation to my high testosterone levels. For example, yesterday I *felt* like buying a soup but buying a soup *was* optionless. I needed it as one of my organic testosterone supplements. So like an oily beaver swimming up the damn, I drove to the family grocery store to get it. It made me think of a certain Sartre who said, "I would like people to remember the milieu or historical situation in which I lived, ... how I lived in it, in terms of all the aspirations which I tried to gather up within myself." Now there's a man who had real hat energy.

10/17

"ON THE ONE HAND, YOU'D BE GREAT IN THAT WIG because you're so self-conscious, and on the other, that's precisely why you'd suck at it." I haven't seen YA in years and am integrating myself back into him like a bag in which leftover beans are temporarily frozen. THAT IS PRECISELY WHY *WE'D* SUCK AT IT, he corrects. Another instance in which YA's remaining lust, the lust of my X, equivocates between pity and friendship (or pity *as* that). Well he never actually saw me standing there in that bright orange wig, that complimentary orange get-up in which I rode the elevator up to LEE's patron-husband's, up to all the other colors who were cheersing at their laps. And if he did, then I wouldn't be so forward-thinking and "*WE*" wouldn't exist. YOU KNOW IF WE DIDN'T BREAK UP, YOU WOULDN'T EVEN BE ABLE TO *THINK* THE WORD "WIG" YOU'D BE SO TIMELESS? A WORTHLESS SPECK OF DUST, A BUG IN A RUG, A WINDLESS SLUMP. IF WE DIDN'T BREAK UP YOU WOULDN'T BE ABLE TO THINK IN TWO STREAMS. WE'D BE GREAT OR WE'D BE DEAD. I'D BE THE CAKE AND YOU'D BE THE BED SOME OTHER HUMAN GOES ON USING–NO BREAKUP POEM TO TELL ABOUT IT.

TODAY

LOOK AT THESE ONIONS, someone says, walking by us while we are dancing. He isn't talking about the kind of onions that burrow, vibrating-ly, into the soil, only to be fully revealed with a cross-section—he's talking about us, the two of us. The man walks by with a really subtle feeling as he says it, like he's using his nail to flick his words off his teeth and into the ground. So I suppose on one level we were integrating into it, our legs pounding into the periodically dusty periodically wet earth, our bare legs. He flicked me into that idea, an iota of it. I, on the one hand, was wearing white gloves with temperature reacting bulbs at the tips of them and a piece of sequined silver fabric plus a silk chemise, while he was tall and carried a ball. To sneeze, I look at white snow. It was the first time in my life I felt the stifled rejection of belonging to a topic in the immediate moment, a category of things kids call kids: ONIONS. Plus, it was 6 AM, which didn't lessen the abject feeling. We weren't even dancing in a proper field or near a proper stage—we were by the porta potties or a food truck just beginning to prepare for breakfast. I couldn't tell if the man wanted to engage in conversation, plus I was too tired to speak even if he had wanted to. So instead of saying, I CAN'T HELP IT THAT

MY DAD LOVES PEOPLE!, I just continued to dance. I made myself more dizzy. I planted myself an orange carrot next to the turquoise porta potties.

10/23

"No, No," I said, "*That's* Father Wilson." I was driving on the tracks at the UNIVERSITY OF SEX AND ORANGES when my brain wanted to say that. I was driving in a car behind a white van that was supposed to carry university students in it, but failed. I could tell because the windows, though outwardly opaque, were just a tiny bit see-through. The only person I could see was the man, the MAN IN THE VAN. Don't ask me why but when I saw him I had the desire to call him something else. Or was it the desire for something hiding, then something revealed, by which I was afflicted? Any one of us would love to imagine one of our leaders living a secret life in which they are employed as a university bus driver. Or was it that I wanted to be proxy to the knowledge that a REAL MAN *was,* in every sense of the term but actual, physical being (as in, *there's always a real president's wife behind him*) this person who, being in the public eye, was given all the actual credit, the REAL MAN having worked for it tirelessly, nobly, and always behind-the-scenes? The REAL MAN and the MAN IN THE VAN have historically had a complicated relationship, though the man I saw was protected from these "darker rabbits" as the sheer blindingness of the sun reflecting off the snow intercepted any allusion to candy. The thought of which

intercepts my fist as it punches
these words individually, like
stereotypes. The original language,
which, before I'd thought of the
white light, its overwhelming audio-
visual impression, was more likely
the cause of my shoving Father in
front of that van.

10/26

I want to marry you but you're not my boyfriend. I want to marry you but you're gay. I want to marry you but I'm not rich. I'm poor, actually, quite the opposite of rich. I'm charging, chagrin, the electrons required to spin a thing into its opposite, to signal and then squeegee the dialectic via watching the reflection of the sun seen from outside my window and reflected back onto my laptop screen, focusing just on the halo outside, just on the thin ring of cirrus clouds made by tiny ice crystals, so that maybe you'll like me, decide, magically, you're not gay? I can tell it's working (I can smell its worth stinking) because the longer I stare, the more I lose the corner of the sphere (yesterday a student Sid said Salvador Dali saved himself from oblivion because of the precision of his lines, but I think they were digitally rendered) to a rapid band of six colors dispersed by a prism, though I can't tell if this is an effect of the eyes, the light, or of my computer's cells visibly splitting. Either way, what I want to say is THIS IS A SACRIFICE, so maybe you will come to like me and not just boys. Is that really how I think? That somebody gives you a ticket and somebody else punches it, says the last words of Edith Pilaf? No, but I will for you, sweet, gay poet! I look at the light, the Christmas lights I bought on Amazon

and hung in my apartment for when
I practice deep yoga stretching,
stop myself from sneezing—my way
of getting back at you. Back to you?
Back to myself? Then my glass eye
crunches all the lumens of Caligula
on purpose.

DAY

I remember the State Farm tent as I remember the Clydesdales: red, and hogging a whole one-third of my vision as a hog hogs the fame from all the other state fair animals. I laid out the problem in the first sentence. It is how can STATE and FARM and (I guess we won't forget him—he's the tail of the oink) TENT go together? There is a contradiction hiding somewhere in there. Or, I guess I shouldn't say *hiding*—it's blatant, it's up-front—but, I think an aspect of it (the size of a third) is shy, coiled like the tail of a pig. It made the festival really good, that whole dynamic. I kept returning to the tent every time I felt things had gotten too mystical or too woodsy (after I got out of the tree I'd fled up when I was being chased by those MAN DOGS, for instance). One night, when a guy from the neighboring camp decided he was too far gone and needed to go to medical, I said, COME ON, GO GET YOUR FLAG and took him to the State Farm tent. They treated him with some bluish-green potion that immediately resolved all apparent contradictions. OUCH, he said, as the drink went down, but only like when you have a toothache.

TODAY

Being with Michael, not being with him, being forever in-between, I am understanding like never before just exactly what writing is. It is transforming insubstance into substance, a kind of bluish, red-flecked-stone-carved-into-the-shape-of-a-scarab alchemy. Like me, writing is unembarrassed creating something out of flecks of dead skin, tiny particles, admixture of ash and wind from the mouth of a fireplace bellows. That smoke that is keeping the faith in absurd and dire circumstances. Like me, writing SHALL REMAIN IN HOPE–shall keep the faith–that natural love and fucking will bring us closer together and will, eventually, make us unstoppable again, for natural love and fucking, my dear, is where we began. I open the letter to write this down for you, but the music stops. A bird wants to rap on my window, but knows, prematurely, it can't get in. This is the sadness of the alchemists no one ever tells, that all the talk of making gold was a way of staving off their final, broken hearts. A symptom of keeping a secret is pretending you are unembarrassed. I mean, have you seen how they dressed?

DAY

Another dream. This one's full of switchback turns. The engine driving is my wishing I had something else. The dream's about my Xs. I dream that there are two. I'm with a current boyfriend (someone... I don't know who... definitely not YA... doesn't have the same Do-It-Yourself Earrings) who I'm trying to slough away like a boa shedding its skin for a newer sheen or like a person, like myself, taking off an itchy, consumptive orange wig. Like the snake, I have to work for it. Ack ack, I'm literally climbing up, ghosting aloft the bland, prescriptive boy I used to be with. I do everything to fight for him, the BOY OF MY FUTURE, the BOY FLOATING ABOVE MY HEAD, the BOY FOR WHOM I ITCH AND ITCH AND CONSUME THIS GROSS BROWN TARRY LIQUID. I do everything, and then, at last, I get there. We are together. Everything is cool and light, light gold and warm. Light. It's copacetic. I'm, how do I put it, excited...

Everything in life, the mind, exists vertically, on the order of all-glass buildings. Beautiful as a point but a little bit scary when you consider all-glass buildings usually just go up and up, without ever converging at a joint. That's what happens to me. That's what happens to my mind. Suddenly, this cloud of a great confusion opens up, and I realize the boy I just fought so hard to get with is *not* my real boy. He is not the one I want. I have forgotten the real one, the one who is the very best. When I see him (the one who is legit), I do so quickly recognize him, but the point of the dream is how I will forget what I know best. How I will deliberately smudge my memory out, like a cloud. Or, how I will settle.

TIME

Crutches don't have to signal death unless you let them. Just like the boy who said it isn't awkward unless you make it. I needed to be carried by the crowd of my new community just like I needed to go to the coffee shop to get work done. My problem was mistaking one letting go for another, in addition to saying the wrong thing. So it was scary when I saw her. Smells heightened, I had the urge to bend a nail, the grocery belt in front of me grew more and more colicky. I was like a baby scared of individuation, individuation having already been achieved, or like a baby who saw individuation as precarity. As NOT GUARANTEED. Probably an effect of my high levels of T. The woman crutched in. She wore a neon pink T-shirt and had a smile like a barge in mid-winter. She smelled like that, too. And, her smell liked it—in other words, she was OK. I wanted to sit with her and tell her *I want to love on you*. I wanted her to know I loved her largesse and that I loved it in the third-person. And I wanted to know better than to want that ever. Instead, I fled in place. I pulled Google up:

GROCERY BAGS CAUSE DISEASE
I look up
GROCERY BELTS CAUSE DISEASE
I look up
JOBS CAUSE DISEASE
I look up

HEISTS CAUSE DISEASE
I look up
WET CEILINGS CAUSE DISEASE
I look up
SHAME CAUSES DISEASE
I look up
COLONIALISM CAUSES DISEASE
I look up
REGENERATION CAUSES DISEASE
I look up
REALISTIC RENDERINGS OF BAMBOO
IN PAINTINGS CAUSE DISEASE
I look up
GOOGLE CAUSES DISEASE
I look up
FOOT-IN-MOUTH DISEASE CAUSES
DISEASE
I look up
FLEEING IN PLACE, I.E., LACK OF
MOTILITY, CAUSES DISEASE
I look up

TIME

I am out in the field. I am in the mild yellow grasses of my backyard— or, what looks like my backyard but might actually be the festival grounds (the grass is a similar brown). A few friends are with me. Just my closest ones. The ones who feel like brothers or sons. We've laid out a tapestry— then, suddenly, there's no more sun. Everything is just gray, and the trees are breaking in the wind, suggesting rain. So many different things are fucking with my sense of smell at once. I have never seen a pre-storm color like this. And I've lived here all my life, to boot. Something bad is about to happen. The homunculus we all consistently pushed down is finally getting its vindication. Then, suddenly, the clouds clear up. And it doesn't rain. The sun returns to the way it looked previously. ISN'T IT AMAZING, says one of my friends (we are so close; he is like my littlest brother). ISN'T IT AMAZING HOW QUICK WE ARE TO JUMP TO THE WORST THING? LIKE THINKING IT'S THE END OF THE WORLD, AS IN JUST NOW? It's weird, because I am somehow more scared of him saying this than I was of the whole eclipse. His utterance feels like a force, lesser than me (at least in age), is ascending a purplish cell tower with me underneath it. Like he came from the future or the past or the dull depths of some buried reality. He spurned my homunculus in a nice way.

TIME

I'm in class. There is a laminate cut-out of a fish on the wall, but no water. Someone says, I THINK THE POST-STRUCTURALISTS WOULD BE HAPPY WITH THAT IMAGE, OF THEIR WORK AS A RABBIT HOLE, BUT ONLY AFTER THEY'RE DEAD (ONLY AFTER THEY'RE DEAD). *Only after they're dead, only after they're dead*, the rest of the students respond, snap-whispering. This whole class starts to feel like a joke bed, and I try to think about why. In trying to comprehend how this class is like a joke on a bed, you have to bring your whole self to it. Lay down on it, like. Let touch, as they say, go touching every crease. THIS IS THE ONLY WAY YOU WILL TRULY UNDERSTAND THE POST-STRUCTURALISTS, the teacher says. "By approaching the ghosts of them head-on, then walking through their ectoplasm." The reason I haven't grasped this yet (why I am the last in the class to join the chorus) is because the whole thing feels too self-focused. Why do *I* have to walk through *their* ectoplasm? I think. Why is the whole thing about *me* laying on a bed to sleep? Why are the *dead* always in the position of the *bed* when we assign a metaphor to their thinking? Then my teacher slaps me. "Your thinking about it is much too general," she says, "as usual." IT'S A RABBIT HOLE. GET IT THROUGH YOUR THICK SKULL. WE DIE BEFORE WE CAN LAUGH AT A TROPE.

TIME

DO YOU REMEMBER BALL PITS? was the last question you asked before we fell out of love with each other. What that question showed, above all, was a kind of ignorance that meant you lacked an understanding not only of what I liked, toward which futures I was bent, but that in you there was a fundamental absence of who I was to me. When you looked in the mirror, you saw thee. Our car was blue and reflected our own images off the windows of the shops we passed. When you said it, I almost sweared a word. The tendon feeding that impulse into my leg and up my spine didn't choke my neck out like a tree but sprained a nerve just a little bit so I was veritably frustrated, though not really enraged. It was all so in-between. I wanted you to understand ball pits in their centrality, or at least to know in them my sex's symmetry (TO POKE MY SOUL THERE) and, at the same time, I wanted to push you far away, to be the only one swimming in that rainbow-plastic, air-filled sea. I WANTED MY SPIRIT TO BE FREE, in other words. I wanted the air trapped within that plastic to finally be able to breathe, and I guess only just now realized this is impossible in toxic relationships. How could I ever thank BALL PITS, my onliest patron saint, for shaking me out of my role-playing of a life? I could've just hired some random guy to drive my car into near-accidents, regularly, and that would've worked just fine.

TIME

I cry in the wrong places with just the right combination of things. Like my family, a crowded deli, and meats. Like the beauty of the chef's singing. I cry whenever I'm hunched over a bog, a log, this counter on which the deli man serves me my food, and I see something beautiful. I cry when the fat chef sings. Which does feel weirdly primal, weirdly like amphibians, their slick skins green against the red of these meats. It feels like A RELEASE. Like Jesus Christ himself were that chef, or rather, like Jesus Christ was using him. O yes. He had no motive of his own. He was like, since the weather's changing now, these flying geese machines, perfectly coiled up (their coils perfectly toiled up) to the breeze between winter and spring. THE BREEZE BETWEEN WINTER AND SPRING BEGETS THE BREEZE BETWEEN WINTER AND SPRING, the chef sang, so fat and I had already started eating at the counter, having just paid for my meal. A line already forming behind me. I sobbed all over my meats and bread. I wanted not to know I required this fuel, to be turbine-powered like the goose. I felt evolved into the inferior position. My mom was somewhere in the room, but I couldn't fathom beauty.

Notes

"8/12":
The phrase "Oppenheim's dorsiflexion of the great toe elicited by irritation downward of the medial side of the tibia" is taken from a Wikipedia article on "Oppenheim's Sign," which takes its definition from: Swartz, Mark H. (2006). *Textbook of Physical Diagnosis: History and Examination With STUDENT CONSULT Online Access. Philadelphia: Saunders. p. 694.*

"9/28":
The excerpted quote by Sartre is from a 1975 interview found in: Charlesworth, Max (1976). *The Existentialists and Jean-Paul Sartre.* University of Queensland Press. p 154.

My sincerest gratitude and thanks to the editors at Spuyten Duyvil, T Thilleman and Aurelia, for their work bringing this book into the world. Special thanks to TT for the cover. Thank you to Diane Seuss and Joyelle McSweeney and to all my teachers and mentors for supporting my work, and to my friends and peers who did the same. Thank you CA Conrad, Vi Khi Nao, and Candice Wuehle for your art and generosity and to the editors at *DIAGRAM* and *Posit* for publishing some of these pages. Thank you to my parents, my family, and all my loves.

ELISE HOUCEK is a writer, artist, and recent graduate of the MFA program at the University of Notre Dame. Her writing has appeared or is forthcoming in *The New Delta Review*, *The Comstock Review, DIAGRAM, Prelude, Posit, Afternoon Visitor, Always Crashing* and other journals and has been supported by residencies from Art Farm and a fellowship from the Pierce Cedar Creek Institute for Environmental Education. Her poetry chapbook, *So Neon Was the Rope*, was a semi-finalist for the 2021 Tomaž Šalamun Prize from *Verse* and will be published by Osmanthus Press in 2022. *TRACTATUS* (Spuyten Duyvil, 2021) is her first "book."

www.ingramcontent.com/pod-product-compliance
Lightning Source LLC
Chambersburg PA
CBHW011406070526
44577CB00003B/392